W9-BHY-478

WITHDRAWN

WITHDRAWN

ANTHOLOGY

Rules of Sleep

Books by Howard Moss

Rules of Sleep

Poems by Howard Moss

New York Atheneum *1984*

Some of these poems originally appeared in magazines to which grateful acknowledgment is made:

ANTAEUS *Upstairs*

DENVER QUARTERLY REVIEW *The Islands* (*The Islands* first appeared in a limited edition published by PALAEMON PRESS LIMITED)

GRAND STREET *Rooftop*

INQUIRY *Form and Content*

THE NATION *The Miles Between*

THE NEW REPUBLIC *Song from the Intensive Care Unit*

THE NEW YORK REVIEW OF BOOKS *Fingerprints, Venice: Still Life*

THE NEW YORKER *Nerves, Mentioning These Things, In Umbria, Rules of Sleep, The Gallery Walk: Art and Nature, The Seasons in New York, No Harm, In Traffic, Upstate, Rome: The Night Before, Making a Bed, The Swimming Pool, The Light Put Out, New Hampshire, The Restaurant Window, Weekend, Einstein's Bathrobe, A Hill*

RARITAN *Morning Glory*

VANITY FAIR *More Lives of the Great Composers*

Copyright © 1984 by Howard Moss
All rights reserved
Library of Congress catalog card number 83–45123
ISBN 0–689–11422–2 (clothbound)
ISBN 0–689–11423–0 (paperback)
Published simultaneously in Canada by McClelland and Stewart Ltd.
Composed and printed by Heritage Printers,
Charlotte, North Carolina
Bound by The Delmar Company, Charlotte, North Carolina
Designed by Harry Ford
First Edition

For Alastair Reid

Contents

V

I

In Umbria

For Daniel Lang

The wrong assumption flirted with the possible:
A grave burst open,
St. Clare's body still in her nightdress
Flying in a vertical rush to Heaven,
Abandoning the stones speechless with sadness.
At first the woods were level, then unreal,
The stars alarmed by a wind shift, moonlight
Startled by the thrill of the extraordinary.
But soon the unexpected settles down,
Settles down, becoming ordinary
In landscapes compelled to tell a story—
Landscapes like this one seen from the tilted
Courtyard in front of the church at Assisi,
The hills peaceful with their fuzzy greenery,
Angels at rest who ask no questions,
And a sky that sails, finally, serenely.

In the church's glassed-in reliquary
A saint's bones give off neither a peculiar
Shining nor any semblance of the human.
Help is coming in this hospital
Of souls where first-aid never arrived
On time before; the holy bandages
Being folded now by hands of mercy
Will let that woman in black rise up
From her wounded knees, that gnarled old man
Believe in the sanctity of the uninjured.

Happy the monks strayed out of history
Walking forward toward the central fountain,
Dry, ornamental, surrounded by grasses.
Only the play of light on the hills,
Captured for good in religious paintings,
Serves as an emblem of the spiritual life
Of Umbria: three syllables of shade—
Or one—cast by a cypress tree
Alone in a field whose brush of thin
Shadow works the sundial of the day;
In this fief of the godly, art
And feeling are as intertwined
As orthodoxy and heresy.

"Far" and "down" are being redefined
In a medieval town up in the mountains.
Which is farther away: the valley
Floor invisible below or the distant
Hillside glimpsed in a haze of ozone—
The horizontal and the vertical
Having lost all meaning? The circle thrives—
The semicircle, rather—of the mountain
From whose rim the houses stacked in stone
Rise up again; a church and fountain
Domesticate a fortress of a town
Where the *gelateria* stays open late
And the park has the charm of the unnecessary.

So civil is it all
That one might be at a luncheon party
Attended by monks in a sunlit courtyard,
Clerics explaining to Swedish tourists
The history of the single Tintoretto
That has kept this monastery alive
Three hundred years. The wood of crucifixion
Lies everywhere about; its subject is either
Bred in the bone, in Umbria, or nothing:
The flowers are heavy with theology,
The birds fly by like Biblical quotations.
In all this shadowy world of sunlight,
In tiers and tiers of arranged hillsides,
Rays of evening fall on the earthworks.
The shades of Umbria are growing darker.

And what the dead have to say today
Is old, old as the hills, a phrase
Meaningless until one stares at these
Great slants of grave sites, reaching up
Always to the light, which the dead can't do,
Whose every particular is shelled to bone;
They say, "Our hearts, too, were full
Of sunlight once. Joy is in the shade.
Look at it. Look. It is beautiful."

The Gallery Walk: Art and Nature

A lesson in perspective, a trick of light?
How to daub some innocent canvas
With the seedy grapeshot of a current fashion?
No, I am only trying to teach you
What pleasure is, and also about
The end of things,
And how the two of them go hand in hand.

To me, music is at the heart of it,
And painting of every kind and school,
From Florence's serene Annunciations—
Mary surprised, not astonished, at the news,
Some angel like a flat-footed bird nearby
Or threshing upward toward a thread of goldleaf,
Blue-green finicky, brushworked hills
Beyond—to Pollock's wounded linoleums
Wriggling away, or Rothko's bars
Of cathedral light. I am also partial
To the monumental:
Sculpture against the ruins of sculpture,
Afternoons in Rome, light everlasting.

Something, too, should be said for the crafts,
The ewers, crocks, cups and saucers
Spread out on tables over centuries
For the altar's royal elegants, or for
The crop dividers coming home at dusk
To share their simple gains and leaves.

Each time among them two figures appear,
Repentant Adam, unknowledgeable Eve,
Boring as ever with the family news,
And always there comes the same surprise:
She falls down in the middle of a joy,
He keels over at the wedding feast,
And then the lament goes on and on,
Witless, without humor, dumbfounded, grim . . .

And so it is better to look at the dancers,
Or these beautiful canvases of dancers dancing,
Or listen to music recreate the pulse
Of sounded, marvellous emotions caught
In the lines of the body, its grace and flights,
And to see on the wing of a violin
Nature soaring in, all green,
A tree, in which a bird will seek
Its habitation the summer long,
Singing its heart out, as usual.

Rome: The Night Before

I
On the terrace of the Villa Aurelia
Overlooking Rome (obscured by trees)
A form of life sprang into being
Too ideal to outlast the moment:
You sunbathing, reading in the sun,
And I flicking dead leaves and dried blooms
From geraniums in terra-cotta pots,
Each looking like a shrunk Napoleon.

We lived high up in Roman air, looked down
On a summer resort of corrugated stone,
Echo and rotunda, footfall, dome—
History turning corners everywhere
As if the faces of the night before,
Random visions of the street, were now
Individually fixed in marble brawn
Or in the cool shade, room on room,
In the Villa Farnesina or the Vatican Museum.

But museums in Rome are tautologies;
The same faces one sees hurrying past
On the streets are up on the walls and there-
Fore doubly visible: the seer and the seen,
With the same elegance at work—its fine
Italian hand springing from a fountain,
Or serving food and wine, its eyes and ears
Listening for birds down by the Tiber
Or watching, along with us, the ocular
Skylight dome of the Pantheon
Catching its round of sun or rain.

2

In the dowdy, magisterial squares
Of sculpture in Trastevere,
What generosities of light and water!
And everywhere the dirt lies underfoot
To prove the human imprint's never lost,
No, not even in the midst of grandeur.

3

How shall the cypress imagine the fuller
Shade of the beech, or the brain design
The once living architecture of the skull?
No watcher of water can bring that moment
In time alive when the first impression
Appears, a dent in marble, the erosion
Of stone by falling water, or the pressure
Of human weight, one plane worn down
A touch each century; a chemical
Film of cancer, working its way in,
Tears at the meat of statues and muddies
The finest Roman torso, Roman profile,
The dribbling-down distortions of the air
Turning a colossus into candle wax.

4

Everything permanent is due for a surprise,
The stopped stunned by the ever-changing.
What everybody always took for granted
Astonishes a second before it disappears,
Like the dinosaur who left a plate of bones
And was gone for good. In Rome one feels
Duration threatened day by day,
Not knowing which of its great works will last,
Flesh and marble the same mix of mortar.

Venice: Still Life

At one of the tourist traps in Venice,
Alone for lunch, I watch a guide's
Innocuous school of fish swim by,
Back up, swirl in, to nibble a bit,
Awash among the famous paintings
Before they head out for the icons—
Shrines whose outlines will dissolve in moonlight.

And where else have life and art become
So utterly as one that this not very good
Meal hastily set before me by a saint
With certain thuglike, endearing thumbs
Might be a still life for all the taste
It has, a still life by a second-rate
Dabbler over for the trade, or glass,

Or to study the artful glaze of still lifes
Hanging on a wall in the watery light
Spewed up from a canal at God knows what
Lucky hour of dispensation: a gleam,
Or a steady mirrorlike glint and flame,
The kind that twilight walks down steps for
Into the crowds of water at its feet.

II

Mentioning These Things

Mentioning these things: a clavichord cover
Closed, its gray-green plank fastened tight
By the scrolled Spanish clasp of two gold hinges,
Its chain a tether on the charms of the baroque;
Across the room a star-struck sprig
Of magnolia stuck in a jar of water—
A crystal shape of light, marred at the top
By pieces of bark that the cut branch sheds,
Scumming the surface with spent bits of life
(Husklike cups enclosing the blossoms
That dry out as they bloom, like those of cotton);
On the terrace two deck chairs seem to invite
The arrival of a painter who is strangely drawn
To another landscape—Chinese mountains, say,
Or a desert whose wildflowers are in bloom;
Since there is nothing here but waiting,
The sun is drawing trembling spider patterns
Of light on the rough yellow stucco of a wall,
In the room a fireplace swept of ashes,
Its hearth scoured clean by a stiff whisk broom,
And, at right angles to a rosewood chest,
A desk is waiting for its poems to light,
The glass door at a slant, the sky aswim
With the clouds and touches of the known unseen.

The Restaurant Window

A time-lapse camera might do it justice,
This street outside the restaurant window,
Feeling hurrying by on one side
And thought on the other.
Gradually night sponges up vision,
A moment so made up of other moments
No one can tell one famous variation
From another. Soon they will become the theme.
It is then that the power of form is felt
(Could it have been, all along, the subject matter?)
Connecting everything, the ginkgo's gesture
And the ginkgo, even permitting
The streetlamp turning on every evening
Its one small circle of illumination,
As if it were reading, over and over,
The same book of poems.

Insurgent sounds of music, bells
Add their bits to the pending structure,
A latent second holding in its spell
The chromatic shift to the second after,
Each table lamp an imitation
Of the light outside, and in the haze,
Part incandescence, part refraction,
Fine distinctions you have never grasped
Swim into view, the elusive becoming
A mute but embodied expectation.

And now as people vanish from the street
(A hurricane lamp outlasting its tempest)
The trees relax into Japanese silence;
Even the glasses assume their true property:
Waiting only to be filled or emptied.
The world's no more than a neutral surround
Until it begins to move with purpose—
Such moments are lived alone: at night
In the white capsule of a hospital room
After the warm visitors have left,
The chill of what is about to happen
Settles between you and a stranger
Walking into the room politely;
Both of you know you are not there for nothing.

Thus this street: it has an ending somewhere,
An event flaring out of sight in the west—
The sunset, already settling for less.

Nerves

Who doesn't have them—bad as the war news
Starting the day off with a little tic,
And you're out of bed, already launched into it,
The announcer stopping to catch his breath
Between two movements of a cello concerto:
"Distant shelling was heard today
In the suburbs of Beirut . . ." What's left of it.
The hungry newsboy touting the death
Of thousands to sell the morning paper . . .
But, no, these are not the true illustrations:
For those, your unique fate is grafted
Onto the general terror, your mirror
Revealing one night in X-ray the tumor
That will kill you, a sudden pain in your chest
Knocking you flat on the bathroom tiles.
And nobody told you the acid rain
Would be fatal today to one who walked
Down to the docks to see the freighters in,
The men in overalls greasing the way
For some new environmental disaster,
A tanker leaking its sick ammonia
Into the Hudson, Liberty at bay,
While last night's hunks of sex weave by,
Still drunk, on their electric rail,
Toward home, wherever those two rooms are
That are dark, though the sun is at the full.

Upstairs

Was it a spray of sunglasses
Suddenly molten forming in drops
That drenched the new construction site
At the end of the street—that cul-de-sac
Of fences dripping with rose scallops

Defining protected real estate?
Upstairs in her room, having an Irish
Sense of sin, Miss Finney guzzled
Down her week's ration of British gin.
The lawn blackened with crows—noisy

Stubs of priests preaching unholy
Doctrines, self-fulfilling omens,
Sackcloth news of the grand finale.
Yet at every garbage heap
Romance skins back its banana peel—

The bride pops up and the frog prince,
And all the old whores of formaldehyde,
Innocent as milk, their eyes wide,
Suffer the groom's inept harangue.
Meanwhile, the park's two gaslit lamps,

Washing forward into a grove of trees,
Announce an opening into doom
Down a steep flight of cement steps;
They are being lit by the wavering hand
Of a coachman whose horse is cold and wet.

How Shall We Live?

How shall we live without the wherewithal,
In hotel lobbies, shopping malls, and Sears?
Sex is animal. Fire is magical.

Power and money, each truly evil,
Spawn new Gonerils and new King Lears—
How shall we live? Without the wherewithal,

Like Humpty Dumpty heading for a fall,
Down and down we go, our knees in tatters.
Sex is animal. Fire is magical.

Live in a bank vault, office, or a cell.
Be quiet. And impassive. Don't shed tears.
How shall we live without the wherewithal?

Hoard your bread and water. Hide the pill
Of nightly shadow you rummage for in drawers.
Sex is animal. Fire is magical.

Beware the mail, the obscene phone call,
The battered moments gathered into years.
How shall we live without the wherewithal?
Sex is animal. Fire is magical.

Fingerprints

Does the café table bear the fingerprints
Of Victor, his transmuted fires gone,
And one more vodka on the waiter's tray?
The trees here smell of zinc. The setting sun
Is dragging its copyright down the sky—
I'm at the bay where nothing ever happens.

And nothing brings back Sally. Nothing can.
Her second marriage doomed, that Indian giver,
Hope, took back the few small crumbs he gave her.
Taking her last shaky look at the river,
Dissolving Nembutal in gin, she swilled
The whole concoction down from a cocktail shaker . . .
Even forms of suicide go out of fashion.

Nikos? Who knows where former Greek gods go.
Into a pantheon out in the Hamptons?
When last seen, he was cadging drinks
At a tourist joint in Maine, then moved from there,
Became a bartender, and then a bar,
Drinking his way from harbor to harbor.

Leslie, if you should rise up from the deep,
Like a diver reversed in a sped-up movie,
Tell me, why did you leave us all for M.
And die beside him in a leaky cruiser
In foul-weather gear in Great South Bay
With a storm coming up, you the best sailor

The boatyard and the Coast Guard ever knew?
Maybe some wise bird passing over
In instinct's annual fall migration
Can fill in all the stories, give them meaning,
Send us a clue or sign we'll understand,
Fall in the leaves, the sky cold blue.

The Seasons in New York

Swordsmen at play have left the sun
Pierced between two West side buildings—

Ah! But what a great recovery!
Here they come again, New York's quick changes:

Alpha the water god floating his skin
Of rainbow scum across a water pond,

Then—presto! chango!—winter's coming in,
The dumb silent animal of snow

Lowering its body over the city,
Suggesting in its camouflage the weight

Of icy paws too heavy to get up.
And now it's spring, or fall, or later:

Hard-edged, the outline of a ziggurat
Walks up its graph into the limelight.

Below: the paunchy waterpaper news
On rainy streets. Above: no moon.

Rooftop

1

Rain, will there ever be enough
For the black-tarred roof
Desiring still to become a mirror,
Ever enough slickness of ice?
Today it felt
In the silvering of its underside
A faint image—someone walking
Across it shuddering to be defined,
But when it tried
To shine, the figure, if it was a figure,
Vanished, leaving the fire escape
Empty without its life of crime,
And so the roof waits for the first appearance
Of anything, even a cloud, the curved
Faraway Saracen moon to light
Its way through this
Long winter of loneliness.

2

If it could hold a star, if some
Summer chair now bare of canvas
Would lend the sure spareness of structure
To its moil of undistinguished blackness,
Then it would make its mark, almost
As famous as the moon.

3
Spring has come, it can tell from the way
The light is leaving the living room,
From the way the beginning is beginning again,
A welling up, then a slackening—
Can a thaw settle in to stay?
Today it knew it was right because
The first light shadow of a leaf was thrown
In exquisite scale across its skin.

4
Does the ice confer
Grace on the skater's heel, the wing
Of a bird become pure speed because
It rises against the motionless?
How the sky shows off its talismans
Enhancing the outline of each thing,
The way the heavens miraculously
Have turned the drabbest skyline tonight
Into the golden ramps of a city
Filled with the spectrum's crisps and chars,
As if some bare Egyptian whittled
A fine gorget to decorate the neck
Of the cat goddess, a net of blazing fire.

III

Rules of Sleep

In the sludge drawer of animals in arms,
Where the legs entwine to keep the body warm
Against the winter night, some cold seeps through—
It is the future: say, a square of stars
In the windowpane, suggesting the abstract
And large, or a sudden shift in position
That lets one body know the other's free to move
An inch away, and then a thousand miles,
And, after that, even intimacy
Is only another form of separation.

No Harm

No harm would walk in and sit down,
I thought, this fifth time trying on
The passionate gloves, the wary shoes,

A sea oblique in the window shades,
And a distant phonograph's music sound
From the next or the next-after-that apartment.

But harm was already gloved and shod
In my feeling for what was never there,
Or was there in some illusionary life

Of the past, its shadow and its substance.
Here, on a strange coast, the foggy mornings
Lift predictably each day at noon,

The colored lights of the nighttime garden
Weaken and go out, the lukewarm pool
Has nothing of the swift embracing hum

Of a good cold sea. The future's apparition
Is here with me. Come closer, closer,
So we can play our roles—human, ghostly.

More Lives of the Great Composers

For, and after, Dana Gioia

I

Maurice Ravel would buy a bag of figs
and eat them greedily on his back porch
in St. Jean de Luz. His aunts were mortified.
"On summer nights great music drives me mad,"
said Richard Wagner to his maid. And yet
tonight across the street a piano plays
arpeggios of steel. On autumn days,
Schubert would work, then take a walk through woods.
Outside the snow is falling steadily,

and more's to come. A man goes by,
resembling Schubert in his great frockcoat
strolling through the autumn woods. Ravel
had relatives who almost drove him mad.
Tchaikovsky said, "If I could love a maid . . . "
In fact, he tried. The girl was mortified.
And yet across the street a piano plays
as if a madman on a summer night
were tearing down the stars on his back porch.

In the snow country, Bartok on a sleigh
rode toward a castle, and a plate of figs
lying on a table by the fire seemed
as fine as greatcoats seen through autumn woods.
Georges Enesco lost his Spanish maid.
"Go back to Barcelona—that back porch!
Ravel's 'Bolero' soon will drive you mad."
"Arpeggios of steel . . . I'm mortified"—
a Juilliard student. "Mine are soft as figs."

"The pentatonic scale? I do not give a fig
for it," Stravinsky said, but no one heard
because across the street a piano played
arpeggios of steel. "I'm mortified,"
said Mozart, "to find my summer nights
mistaken by the critics for a light snowfall."
Couperin felt, one autumn day, quite mad,
dreamt of his maid, and woke—"That poor old girl!"
"I regret nothing," said Maurice Ravel.

2

"Small talk isn't Ludwig's kind of thing,"
said Beethoven's nephew Karl to Meyerbeer.
Replied that jolly meister, "So I gather,"
though some say what he said was "So I hear."
"*Am* I doomed to be an orchestrator?"
asked Rimski-Korsakov. There was no reply.
"Such minstrelsy arises from the sea,
I think I'll orchestrate it." Claude Debussy.

"La Mer" revives the small talk of the sea,
its great-depth grandeur and its coast small beer.
"You take some jolly-meister orchestrator,
and play a Bach cantata for him, and you'll see
his face go blank with admiration. Me?
Oh, I rise early and stroll beside the sea,"
said Respighi to de Falla. There was no reply.
"I think I'll poison Mozart." Salieri.

Madame von Meck, writing to Tchaikovsky:
"Why don't I hear from you?" There was no reply.
Domenico Scarlatti walked beside the sea
and found the shoreline's foamy beer not jolly.
"Herr Goldberg, I'm feeling very sleepy." Bach.
"I am a great pianist." Paderewski—
"A good cadenza always makes me cry."
"I love the oboes' small talk." Offenbach.

"Sleepy, Herr Schumann?" asked Clara, softly—
she had a date with someone by the sea;
she played Chopin, then Brahms—three intermezzi—
to help along the sandman. There was no reply.
Said Proust to Debussy, "Though minstrelsy
arises from the sea—and *yours* is heavenly—
the world doesn't orchestrate our wishes neatly,
or so we gather as the years go by."

The Miles Between

Ambassador of rain to the night snow,
Custodian of all the miles between,
Who brought the morning tray of light and shadow,
Emissary sun, editing each form,
Illusion's minister who prints the leaf,
Goldsmith of autumn, and you, greenhorn
Conjuror of shoreline and sea storm,

The past's long unforgotten amateur,
Tearstruck highbrow, touchy and extreme,
Reaching for the heights to climb but one,
Soulmate looking for a place to lie,
By the talented flow of Iceland's lava,
By darkness coming down on Hungary,
I swear that you and I will meet again.

Song from the Intensive Care Unit

The dawn takes twenty thousand years
To creep up to my windowsill.
I had two pills to calm my fears,
And for my pain the usual.

Terror, shame, who seeks you out
At the four corners of my room?
The razor teeth of what small mouth
Begin to nibble at my name?

The Light Put Out

For Charles Wright

1

Expected twilight in the flies and wings
Was slow to learn its lines, but once it did,

Nothing could stop the evening's performance,
Suggesting a hand had slipped from the lightboard,

And when the outlines of the trees grew faint,
The background of the outlines fainter still,

Pain, which grows more intense at nightfall,
Occupied its theatre once again—

A chain-link fence of oblate light
The pool kept shaking and repairing.

2

Blinking rapidly to gain once more
The bric-a-brac of the taken for granted—

That common delusion of the mad, or those
About to disappear from the general view—

Looking out from behind a piece
Of wrought-iron, medieval armor, and

Dropping clinkers every time I winked,
I began the phone calls out of the dark.

3
Is that you, Long John Silver, at last?
Dragging your booty across the sill,

A star behind you like a little, burned
Fried potato stuck to the sky?

Nothing will pry it loose. Not even
Soaking. A spatula. Or time.

It's gone, it's back, like a ping-pong ball
Riding on top of the words at a movie.

You know all about it, One-Patch Pirate,
Opening your treasure. Light! All light!

4
A candle-bearer comes with bits of moon
And scrapes the specks of wax into the river.

They float under the eyelid of the sky
Reflected back as clouds on the water.

The birds are trying to teach rocks to fly—
Ungainly students of the night mirror!

5

A veil netted with black dots falls,
Dropping in coals in oil, black wells,

Flies not to be whisked away.
The free-for-all of the night winks on

Somewhere in the distance, more heard than seen
From here—a peculiar shade or screen

Feeling its way to a kind of vision
Alternate as dusk which has no reason

Not to go on to a conclusion affecting
The diners on the terrace rising to go

As well as the stranded traveller several
States away who is leaving the coughing

Hump of a bad used car to get help.

The Summer Thunder

Now the equivocal lightning flashes
Come too close for comfort and the thunder
Sends the trembling dog under the table,
I long for the voice that is never shaken.

Above the sideboard, representation
Takes its last stand: a small rectangle
Of oak trees dripping with a painted greenness,
And, in the foreground, a girl asleep

In a field who speaks for a different summer
From the one the thunder is mulling over—
How calm the sensuous is! How saintly!
Undersea light from a lit-up glen

Lends perspective an arranged enchantment,
As peaceful as a Renaissance courtyard
Opened for tourists centuries after
Knights have bloodied themselves with doctrine.

Making a Bed

I know how to make a bed
While still lying in it, and
Slip out of an imaginary hole
As if I were squeezed out of a tube:
Tug, smooth—the bed is made.
And if resurrections are this easy,
Why then I believe in all of them:
Lazarus rising from his tomb,
Elijah at the vertical—
Though death, I think, has more than clever
Household hints in mind and wants
The bed made, once, and for good.

IV

Einstein's Bathrobe

I wove myself of many delicious strands
Of violet islands and sugar-balls of thread
So faintly green a small white check between
Balanced the field's wide lawn, a plaid
Gathering in loose folds shaped around him
Those Princeton mornings, slowly stage-lit, when
The dawn took the horizon by surprise
And from the marsh long, crayoned birds
Rose up, ravens, maybe crows, or raw-voiced,
Spiteful grackles with their clothespin legs,
Black-winged gossips rising out of mud
And clattering into sleep. They woke my master
While, in the dark, I waited, knowing
Sooner or later he'd reach for me
And, half asleep, wriggle into my arms.
Then it seemed a moonish, oblique light
Would gradually illuminate the room,
The world turn on its axis at a different slant,
The furniture a shipwreck, the floor askew,
And, in old slippers, he'd bumble down the stairs.
Genius is human and wants its coffee hot—
I remember mornings when he'd sit
For hours at breakfast, dawdling over notes,
Juice and toast at hand, the world awake
To spring, the smell of honeysuckle
Filling the kitchen. A silent man,
Silence became him most. How gently
He softened the edges of a guessed-at impact
So no one would keel over from the blow—
A blow like soft snow falling on a lamb.
He'd fly down from the heights to tie his shoes

And cross the seas to get a glass of milk,
Bismarck with a harp, who'd doff his hat
(As if he ever wore one!) and softly land
On nimble feet so not to startle. He walked
In grandeur much too visible to be seen—
And how many versions crawled out of the Press!
A small pre-Raphaelite with too much hair;
A Frankenstein of test tubes; a "refugee"—
A shaman full of secrets who could touch
Physics with a wand and body forth
The universe's baby wrapped in stars.
From signs Phoenicians scratched into the sand
With sticks he drew the contraries of space:
Whirlwind Nothing and Volume in its rage
Of matter racing to undermine itself,
And when the planets sang, why, he sang back
The lieder black holes secretly adore.

At tea at Mercer Street every afternoon
His manners went beyond civility,
Kindness not having anything to learn;
I was completely charmed. And fooled.
What a false view of the universe *I* had!
The horsehair sofa, the sagging chairs,
A fire roaring behind the firescreen—
Imagine thinking Princeton was the world!
Yet I wore prescience like a second skin:
When Greenwich and Palomar saw eye to eye,
Time and space having found their rabbi,
I felt the dawn's black augurs gather force,

As if I knew in the New Jersey night
The downcast sky that was to clamp on Europe,
That Asia had its future in my pocket.

V

To the Islands

Afflicted by order, the minimalist disease,
We leave for the islands and something wilder,
The ocean simmering, reading Jean Rhys
By hurricane lamp in a cottage the builder

Forgot to finish. Or he ran out of money.
At least it isn't dirty, old New York,
Crunch and siren. And when we get lonely,
Bird watching, a phonograph, a nature walk

Come to the rescue. But the ship shipwrecks
On rocks unforeseen. The sun won't come out.
Old standbys don't work, like drink, or sex,
Boredom a poison with no antidote,
And just when we think of getting the hell out,
The beautiful scapegoats arrive by boat.

Weekend

Fridays, executives flock to their châteaux,
Tame as sad behavioral trainees,
The train moving in stupendous twilight,
The rocks of the Hudson at the left, its violet
Tides measured by an unseen moon, when
Suddenly the car penetrates darkness
Ever growing blacker, and is suddenly released
To a few stars trilling, the first virtuoso
Shift of light and, ahead, there it is:
The old train station built for a few
Estates, landowners tucked among the hills,
And for others, escaping from town, a taxi
Leisurely waits because it always knew
The great province of hotels is sleep.

Upstate

Graceful every tuck of the hills
For a stretch until the lopsided barn,
Abandoned hayrick, and broken silo
Make clear once again that Paradise
Is a place that must be left behind.
But, oh, how the hand yearns to make tall
The toppled, how the imagination fashions
Blueprints of former and future perfections—
Weedless gardens where everything blooms
On time and nothing attacks new growth
For its own subsistence. But the eye wanders
From the large to the small, the mind takes in
Only a single slice at a time,
And soon some other natural, wayside
Beauty cancels out thought, and we
Are riding through real and imagined hills
We think will be there forever because
We will be there forever. Our bland

Partnership's ever renewable passions
Roll along with their threatening qualms,
Their long and short endowments of worry,
But, by and large, we work, like the farm
We stared at: green hacked out of hardpan,
Acres of vegetables set in rows,
Rib-swaying, ancient, rust horses calmly
Chewing their way through middle-sized grass,
Its hutches, workable fields, and porch,
On which, way back among the trees,
Someone is silently watching us pass.

New Hampshire

1
When the loons cry,
The night seems blacker,
The water deeper.

Across the shore:
An eyelash-charcoal
Fringe of pine trees.

2
The lake reflects
Indefinite pewter,

And intermittent thunder
Lets us know

The gods are arriving,
One valley over.

3
After the long
Melancholy of the fall,
One longs for the crisp
Brass shout of winter—

The blaze of firewood,
The window's spill
Of parlor lamplight
Across the snow.

4
Flaring like a match
Dropped in a dry patch,
One sunset tells
The spectrum's story.
See the last hunter's
Flashlight dim
As he hurries home
To his lighted window.

Form and Content

1 *Form: The Ice Storm*

Mysteries, once puzzling, become in time
Too literal or genial—that is the end
Of romantic love, and a serious blow
To literary criticism. The work in hand,
Too well formed, starts to nod in the corner
(The badly formed is already fast asleep),
While snow keeps falling, and wild arpeggios
Connect one tree to another in an ice storm;
Then the trapped, bent tops of the stripling
Birches need to be released; heads up,
They're free verse writers once again
As all the world goes fluent in the sun.

2 *Content: The Explosion*

Some of the surroundings look bombed-out,
Ghost apartments staring at the night,
Exploded handbags, their stricken contents
The remains of now unimaginable fates,
Strewn across the rubble and the tarmac,
Yet no one is around, neither the victors
Nor their victims, and, if rumor's to be believed,
Barbarians mass at the city gates.

In Traffic

Even if the highway had been moved to dance,
the stalled traffic, stuck in a line,
choreographed into something interesting—
Chevettes flying sideways in a field,
or up, up into a cloudless sky
where so much space cries out for movement—
still the Real would be on to us again
on this narrow trap of a road adorned with
a diner, a garage, and a nursery,
its trees struggling to produce more leaves.

How gradual spring is here! How impatient
all of us are to be getting home,
as if home were some sort of transfigured instant.
We're stymied, as usual, by the unknown—
a broken-down truck up ahead, an accident,
a Harvester dragging gigantic claws
too wide for one lane, or an animal
refusing to budge—and we begin to wonder
who we all are: the anonymous
taking on interest, the way a tree
stands out suddenly, exempt from its species.

Nothing is really dancing except
an insect or two, whose lives will be smashed
against a windshield once we begin
to move, which we're beginning to do;
a truck full of trees is carting its garden
away toward somebody's landscaped Eden,
and we're picking up speed, single file,
driving past ponds displaying their steadfast
green, through towns too pretty to be.

The Swimming Pool

Once in, this expensive rectangle
Of blue, not quite the Caribbean,
Clear as a filtered tropical-fish tank,
Made going to the beach a dead issue.

A bay crowned with a bridge, a pond
Dammed overnight couldn't be more stunned
Than this sandy hole suddenly marine
Whose constant hum of plumbing soothes

An Atlantic uncluttered by waves and freed
Of a lifelong addiction to salt. Low tides
Bubble away in respective skimmers
Constantly doling out chlorine. A cloud,

Reflected less than a fathom deep,
Is surprised by the American way of life:
"So *this* is gardening," it says to itself,
Admiring free-form tendencies—its own

Ability to be both lamb and lion.
You who will be a shade of nature soon,
Look up—the now felled trees swim by
Casting a shadow by their very absence,

Just as in the city the opposite occurs:
Acetylene torches tear up time
As one more girder is hammered into space,
Wounding the sky with yet another spire.

But here, on this delusive Côte d'Azur,
Something festive and childish has been added
To the scenery—a waterfront of sorts:
This Mediterranean in a matchbox,

Whose lanes are meant for short Olympic laps,
Promises crowds arriving for imagined
Meets, the deck alive with oohs and ahs,
A latticework of lights plying the surface,

And, compliments of small bodies of water,
Birds flying in from everywhere in droves,
The seeds of wild thyme in their beaks,
With credit ratings from all over.

A Hill

For James Fennell

Hacked out of sandy soil to make a pool
    A new outcropping left a shelf of roots—
Ungainly razor cuts, whacked scissor shavings,
    A haircut of the awful lacking both
The plain and crooked virtue of the natural
    And the studied beauty of a formal landscape.
We made a hill of it, brought topsoil in
    Uprooted rhodos and transplanted them
To form a marginal crest, and tamped
    The whole thing down into a rolling dune.
But it is still all stone and earth out there,
    Less loam than a sandy grout for rocks
The glacier left in one haphazard fling,
    A wild thing wanting to get back to wilderness
No matter how we try to tame it with a green
    Wig of fan-junipers, dwarf spruces, yew,
And violets we hope will take, their roots spread nets
    To hold the whole oncoming wave together.

Miami Beach

Was Nature always a snob,
Distributing shorefronts only to the rich?
The poor have come to the right conclusion.

The car lots are dangerous, boutiques have closed
In the cleancut shopping mall whose potted palms
Stand helplessly guarding smashed flower boxes,

As slowly expensive logos drift away;
Subversively dreaming of the cold, signs crumble;
The place has the effect of a dead casino.

Yet the sea repeats its fire drill,
The waves coming in as they were meant to come,
All hailing light, beachcombers, tourists, one

Canadian spinster on her towelled maple,
A lifeguard selling products for the sun—
Still more arrive to take those heat waves in.

If you're high up enough to witness it,
This city's saving grace is light on water,
The bay on one side, the ocean on the other,

Collins Avenue strung out on lights—
Blue neon, the sign language of Paris—
Seen from a terrace overlooking Bal Harbour,

Though this evening's tropical aroma
Is marred by a sad old man who stands regretting
His waistline before a men's shop window,

Watching a coastline glassily reflected
Take its revenge, the tides undermining
The palmed investments of the big hotels,

Breaking through the breastwork of the dunes,
Thundering in to where they used to be,
To lap at the imported Louis Quinze

Already stricken with the plague of mold
Shifting on deer feet in draperied lounges
(So far no one has noticed the ugly

Patch of dry rot under the sofa,
Not even the Cuban trained in mildew,
Trained to pronounce the "doll" in "dollar,"

Otherwise it sounds too much like "dolor.")
How botched is Paradise, how gone for good
Old rock and beach, this gorgeous littoral

Of palms adoring the sun, and sea grape,
Oleander, and white jasmine blooming
Under the nursing home's blinded windows

Where the cardiacs and the sun-stroked blackouts
Wheel past the splash of a tropical-fish tank
Leading a murderous life of its own.

A watering hole abandoned by the young,
Either the old will take it over
Completely or South American money

Found its new capital: a kitsch Brasilia
Of pre-stressed concrete with its air-conditioned
Swiss bank branch, and a single restored

Art deco hotel for absentee landlords
Scanning the sea rehearsing endlessly
Its threatened drama never to be performed.

Morning Glory

For Lee Krasner

Its wrinkled foreskin, twisting open, opens
The silky membrane of a French umbrella;
Within the lighted tent of the corolla
A five-ribbed shape (starfish invention!)
Supports, at the sun's behest, by tension
The small filament plumb at the center.

How blue is blue, how deft the manufacture
Of nature to define a color in a flower,
Balloon, trumpeter, and mountain climber
Among green hearts diagonally placed
In a matching, alternately rising pattern
On the overreaching wire of a stem

Always trying to ensnare another,
A string, anything, as long as it's above—
Chicken wire, trellis, fence rail, nail—
As if transcendence were simply a matter
Of going up and up, and up until
There's no place left in the world to go.

Howard Moss

Howard Moss is the poetry editor of *The New Yorker.*
Before joining its staff in 1948, he was an instructor
of English at Vassar College. The author of eleven
books of poems and three books of criticism, *The Magic
Lantern of Marcel Proust, Writing Against Time,* and
Whatever Is Moving, he has also edited the poems of
Keats, the nonsense verse of Edward Lear, a
collection of short stories written by poets, *The
Poet's Story,* and *New York: Poems,* an anthology.
A play, *The Folding Green,* was first produced
by The Poets' Theatre in Cambridge, Massachusetts,
and then by The Playwrights' Unit in New York
City, and a more recent work, *The Palace at 4 A. M.,*
was produced in the summer of 1972 at the John
Drew Theater in East Hampton, directed by
Edward Albee. In the same year, Moss received the
National Book Award for his *Selected Poems.* In 1974,
he published a book of satirical biographies, *Instant
Lives,* with drawings by Edward Gorey. Moss received
a grant in creative writing from The American Academy
and Institute of Arts and Letters in 1968 and was
elected to its membership in 1971. In 1983, he was the recipient
of a Brandeis University Creative Arts Citation in Poetry, and,
in 1984, a National Endowment for the Arts Award.

PS 3525 .08638 R8
Moss, Howard, 1922-
Rules of sleep

SS $12.95   J44860

MAY 5 '86

1 ① 4/97   3 2/99

Please Do Not Remove Card From Pocket

YOUR LIBRARY CARD

may be used at all library agencies. You
are, of course, responsible for all materials
checked out on it. As a courtesy to others
please return materials promptly. A service
charge is assessed for overdue materials.

The SAINT PAUL PUBLIC LIBRARY